POEMS
TO NIGHT

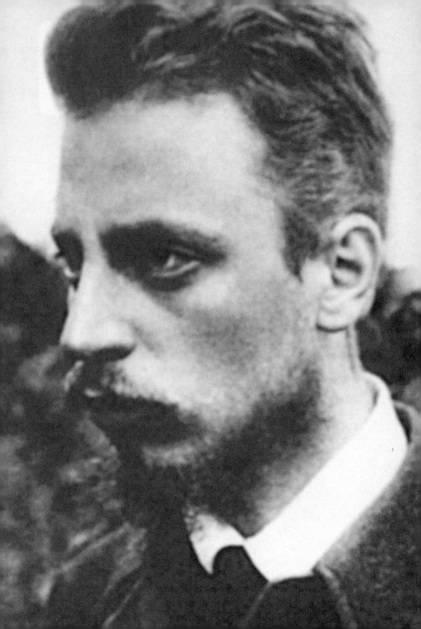

POEMS TO NIGHT

Rainer Maria Rilke

Edited, Translated and with an Introduction by Will Stone

PUSHKIN PRESS
LONDON

Pushkin Press
71–75 Shelton Street
London WC2H 9JQ

First published by Pushkin Press in 2020

3 5 7 9 8 6 4

ISBN 13: 978-1-78227-553-4

These translations were realised with the assistance
of the Fondation Rilke, Sierre Switzerland

Designed and typeset by Tetragon, London

Printed and bound in Great Britain by TJ Books Limited,
Padstow, Cornwall on Munken Premium White 80gsm

www.pushkinpress.com

I believe in Night...

RILKE

(from *The Book of Monkish Life*, 1899)

CONTENTS

LIST OF POEMS

Poems to Night

9

Poems to Night: Drafts

Further Poems and Sketches around the Theme of Night

ACKNOWLEDGEMENTS

I would like to acknowledge the generous assistance of Brigitte Duvillard, Director of the Fondation Rilke in Sierre, who arranged a residence at the Villa Ruffieux in the Château Mercier above Sierre during June/July 2019, to enable me to work on these translations. I should also like to express my gratitude to writer and critic Bruce Mueller in San Francisco for his valuable contributions around Rilke's biographical details, travel itineraries and publishing history. Lastly, I must give fulsome thanks to Linden Lawson, friend and editor, whose suggestions and editorial input have proved invaluable and have served to maintain this translator's foothold at precarious moments on the path.

ⅹ

These translations were realized with the assistance of the Fondation Rilke, Sierre, Switzerland.

INTRODUCTION

At the end of 1916, Rainer Maria Rilke presented the writer Rudolf Kassner, his friend and confidant, with a notebook containing twenty-two poems which bore the title *Gedichte an die Nacht* (*Poems to Night*). These poems, linked by the recurring theme of night, were copied out in Rilke's hallmark meticulous hand. Ernst Zinn, compiler of Rilke's *Sämtliche Werke* (*Collected Works*) [Insel 1992], tells us in his notes that the *Poems to Night* were written between January 1913 and February 1914. What makes them significant is that they were created at the same time as Rilke's most renowned work, the *Duineser Elegien* (*Duino Elegies*), whose eighth elegy Rilke dedicated to Kassner, and reveal correspondences to its genesis as well as anticipating its structure and ushering in new psychic and linguistic territories. In fact, Rilke had originally considered adding the night poems to form a second section of the *Elegies*.

Themes and ideas which run through the *Elegies* are also to be found in the *Poems to Night*; yet unlike the *Elegies* they are more actively hermetic, as if enfolding into themselves and thus demanding of the reader an even greater concentration. The *Poems to Night* possess the aura of a clandestine text, and resist any assured interpretation. Despite their centrality to Rilke's spiritual trajectory, their transcendental disguise, that cosmological searching for the self, has ensured they have remained at the outer margins of his oeuvre, where the poetry-reading public rarely travel. Having said that, a good number of the *Poems to Night* have been translated over previous decades by a range of translators, especially the poem sometimes known as "The Great Night", which begins with the line, "Often I gazed at you in wonder". However, the twenty-two poems have never appeared in English before in their entirety, as they were transcribed for Kassner, but only as odd poems or at best in modest groupings in selections of Rilke's poems. Thus they have never been read as a sequence from beginning to end contained in one volume, nor have a number of ancillary poems and fragments by Rilke on the subject of night dating from different periods been assembled as here, in a supplementary section.

The *Duino Elegies* were conceived and initiated at Castle Duino on the Adriatic coast north-west of Trieste, where Rilke was a guest of Princess Marie of Thurn und Taxis.

The first two elegies were composed early in 1912, and through 1913 Rilke laboured on the material which would become the third, sixth and tenth elegies. The first of the *Poems to Night* were composed in Spain in January and February 1913, but most were written later that same year. It is no surprise to learn that in the autumn of 1913 Rilke was completing the third elegy, which he had begun in 1912 and which shares motifs and elements with the *Poems to Night* and occupies the same nocturnal realm. After the third elegy Rilke struggled to maintain his creative momentum, a state of stasis that was greatly exacerbated in autumn 1914 by the ensuing conflict in Europe. However, care must be taken not to oversimplify the correlation with the *Elegies* and to see things that may in fact not be there, for although the meaning of night in the *Poems to Night* appears sometimes to echo that of the angel in the *Elegies*, at other times in the poems it seems to suggest an altogether different permutation. The reader, then, should approach these poems with an awareness of their ambivalence, of seeming variances of thought, interrelating surges of the objective and subjective which cannot be readily explained, other than by a few detractors as caprice.

In his *Poems to Night*, as elsewhere, Rilke is not philosophizing per se, but loosing strands of thought and ideas that ebb and flow and finally affix to the vertebrae of his lyricism, gifted to us as images; however, this poet studiously eschews any final declaration, any coherent position. Neither is Rilke a poet who offers an absolute poetry, something visibly constructed from a purely metaphysical design. Instead of a system or framework there is only a noble bid for transcendence beyond a finite reality through fluid and pliable poetic utterance, and the arcane aura, the almost organic indecipherability that seems to cloak the *Poems to Night*, serves to underline this. But the *Poems to Night* do not only possess a spiritual linkage to the *Duino Elegies*: it can also be argued that they look backwards, first to the existential desolation of *Die Aufzeichnungen des Malte Laurids Brigge* (*The Notebooks of Malte Laurids Brigge*, 1910) and still further to the presence of the angel in *Das Stundenbuch* (*The Book of Hours*, 1905).

As Anthony Stephens suggests in his *Rainer Maria Rilke's "Gedichte an die Nacht": An Essay in Interpretation* (Cambridge University Press, 1972), the period of the *Poems to Night* is principally one of crisis for their author. Stephens explains that Rilke's journey to Spain at the end of 1912 had initially appeared to provide the inspiration and energy he needed to make a dash for the summit of the *Elegies*, begun earlier that same year; but for reasons which are unclear there was a collapse in confidence, a breaking of the spell, and by the time Rilke wrote the first of the *Poems to Night* in Ronda in the new year of 1913, he was dispiritedly confined to base camp and a sense of dislocation and despair had set in. Stephens explains that most of the subsequent poems were written in Paris, however: "The city itself does not figure in the poems. Rather, it becomes a place of isolation, a kind of no-man's-land in which the relation of self to world is explored without the rich allusiveness and décor of the *Duino Elegies* and *Die Sonette an Orpheus* (Sonnets to Orpheus). There is the 'Ich', the night, the angel, the 'Geliebte' (The Beloved) and very little else." Stephens posits that the period of the *Poems to Night* ends when Rilke met Magda von Hattingberg, or, as she was known to him, Benvenuta, early in 1914. In the poems to Benvenuta, Rilke seems consciously to reject the atmosphere of those of the previous year, and yet the darker material in the essay *Puppen* (*Dolls*), written in February 1914, tells a different story. The precise nature of Rilke's creative configuration in this period remains contradictory and elusive. For example, the poem "Wendung" ("Turning Point"), written in June 1914, has been seized on as proof that Rilke was announcing a new beginning, but this may well be premature. Unfortunately, the sudden trauma of the war three months later means we will never know whether Rilke would have exploited this new beginning, celebrated in that poem and in his more upbeat letters to Benvenuta, or not. What cannot be doubted is that Rilke's personal crisis was extenuated and compounded by the outbreak of hostilities in August 1914. Like many European writers that August, such as his friend Stefan Zweig adrift in Belgium, Rilke was trapped in Bavaria as the once-fluid borders rapidly solidified and he was unable to return to France. Paris and his possessions were out of reach and Rilke relocated to Munich, leaving everything behind in the French capital, including valuable manuscripts and books. In September 1915 he was horrified to learn that they had been sold and dispersed. The psychic strain he suffered in this period is manifest in his correspondence of the time, as well as in the few short texts he dedicated to the war. Yet even in 1915, as the destructive scale of the conflict sank in, Rilke managed to compose the fourth elegy and gamely sought to restore the creative impetus of 1913. This period of disorientation, self-doubt and incertitude lies behind the presentation of the *Poems to Night* to Kassner, as Rilke seeks to reassure a long-standing friend of the continuation of his creative endeavour even amidst the protracted periods of silence and inactivity, the brutal disconnection within the European family as nationalist jingoism strangled pluralism and tolerance. The metamorphosis Rilke regarded as necessary to extricate himself from this depressing period of limited cultural interaction and inner stagnation is famously elucidated in the ninth elegy, "What, if not transformation, is your deepest purpose."

With the *Poems to Night* Rilke offered Kassner a provisory cycle of poems whose mesmerizing sublimity, lyrical reach and spiritual complexity seem to point to the aspiration for a new thematic collection on the lines of *The Book of Hours* or *Das Buch von der Armut und vom Tode* (*The Book of Poverty and Death*, 1905). The presence of night had haunted the poet since his earliest experience of Paris, the period of the *Neue Gedichte* (*New Poems*, 1907) and *The Notebooks of Malte Laurids Brigge*, and was still vital during Rilke's final months in the Valais, as can be seen in the second part of this collection. Rilke's work has a clear antecedent in that of Hölderlin, but also draws on *Hymnen an die Nacht* (*Hymns to the Night*, 1800) by Novalis, that most mystical of German Romantic poets. In these six prose poems interspersed with verse, Novalis celebrates night as a means to gain entry to a higher realm in the presence of God. But although Rilke's own hymns to night evoke his forebear, it is important to remember that Rilke is a poet writing in the era of modernism, only a year before the most murderous war in history swept away a generation and already God had been declared extinct, or at least absent without leave. Rilke treats night as the ultimate terrain for self-becoming, or rather self-securing. The vastness and unknowable nature of night is placed against the individual's finiteness, where the self is constantly threatened with losing purchase on that greater being which binds us as humanity. We underestimate the spiritual governance of night at our peril. However, other factors come into play: the darker hue of Rilke's poetic material was also certainly influenced by his recent peregrinations in Spain. Rilke set off to explore the historic locations of Spain in the hope of bridging the impasse in his creative inspiration, but the encounter with a strange land only served to increase his sense of alienation; "for every journey, above all one through Spain, demands a certain inner equilibrium, but at every moment the world breaks in on me, into my very blood, and all around is strangeness, an unrelenting strangeness." Rilke's willed immersion in its turbulent history and dark legends, his close readings of the Spanish mystics as well as the crucial encounter with the Koran, bled into the poems and fused into the arcane boundless depths of night. In Ronda, a place he had never even heard of and visited on a whim, he finally achieved the balance he sought and began to write; the result was the first of the *Poems to Night*, in terms of chronology, the so-called "Spanish Trilogy", created between December 1912 and January 1913, whose Part I begins, "Out of this cloud, see: the one that so wildly obscures".

Unlike the grander, more declarative *Elegies*, the *Poems to Night* tend hypnotically to reiterate a symbolic theme, a single meditation, through variant images around the mystery of being and the sense of man becoming exposed to the higher lessons of this mystery, and his self-becoming enabled through mastery of the resulting space. Night appears in manifold guises as this space expressly reserved for transcendence, as a force of nature, as helper to man, a guide, a seer. Night itself becomes the visionary from history:

> Does the night not blow cool,
> splendidly distant,
> moving across the centuries.

But night is also threatened by humankind, as here in the opening poem:

> And night has withdrawn into the rooms
> like a wounded beast, in pain through us.

The *Poems to Night* begin to feel like something closer to an incantation, with its endless invocation of space, angel, stars, mouth, moon… images reconstituting, overlapping and morphing. The German word for face, *Gesicht*, is most prominent but slips in and out of various meanings, sometimes seeming closer to "features" and at other times "face", a restless equivocation which Rilke appears to have encouraged throughout. Klaus E. Bohnenkamp, editor of the most recent German edition of *Gedichte an die Nacht* (Insel Verlag, 2016), sees the angel as bridge between the self and night's cosmic enclosure: "In the *Poems to Night* the angel acts as an anthropomorphic figure, link and mediator between human, night and world space." But perhaps the real mediator between self and night is the poem itself, as noted by Charlie Louth in his *Rilke: The Life of the Work* (Oxford University Press, 2020). Of the poem "Overflowing skies of squandered stars" he interestingly suggests: "The poem is a membrane between the self and the night, a tentative contour or interface which in trying to make out a possible relation, in seeking to situate our place in the world, creates not a 'revelation of being', but an 'aperture upon being'." Infinite as the night and stars, the desire of man and of the shadowing angel travel in constant flux, moving towards and away from one another, in perpetual momentum, each serving to shape their role in the mystery of the unknown.

Night has a long history of being commonly ascribed to states of religious or mystical consciousness, yet it exists right there before us, making its presence known with unswerving reliability, and for Rilke it represents a celestial gateway or enacting space between inner and outer reality, or the enclosure within which the self may, if courageous enough, extend from the earthly. As mentioned previously, the idea of night as space for transcendence can be traced back to *The Book of Hours* as a state of inwardness around man's proximity to God, or to *Das Buch der Bilder* (*The Book of Images*, 1906), where night is exulted as the location or the moment when a sublime connection between the self and the external world is forged. But time has elapsed between these earlier collections and the period of the *Elegies*; Rilke has experienced Paris, the modern metropolis, and written his *Notebooks of Malte Laurids Brigge*, and there is a radical shift in his vision of his own existence, his attitude towards God and the objective world. Rilke is not writing in the period of Romanticism or on the back of it: his demanding master is always a modern consciousness. Having said this, we cannot know the extent to which the poet's own life course and its mental challenges infected the imagery of the *Poems to Night*, as Anthony Stephens affirms: "For by and large we simply lack precise knowledge of what correspondences or differences there may be between the poems. We cannot determine to what extent a poem such as 'The Great Night' may be a factual record of a single 'existential moment', whether it is an amalgam of a large number of different personal experiences or to what degree any actual experience may have been modified by the poetic imagination to produce what we encounter in the poem."[*]

Yet what remains undeniable in this tantalizing web of confusion and enigma is that something significant dwells here, something of permanence, a clear sense of the sacred hovers palpably over these poems whatever their connective tissue, Rilke's personal trials and the outflow from previous works. To seek consistency and reinforcement of a theme in Rilke's poetic oeuvre is to attempt to net shadows, for it is this ephemeral design which allows the poet to keep his vision malleable, on the move, to continually question and divine possibilities, to reach out, but not smother what he seeks as soon as he

[*]   Anthony Stephens, *Rainer Maria's Gedichte an die Nacht: An Essay in Interpretation* (Cambridge University Press, 1972).

encounters it, for catching a glimpse is enough. As Rilke writes in the poem "Nocturnal Walk", composed in Capri in 1908: "And whoever knows too much / the eternal will slip away from." The *Poems to Night* confirm that it is this willed ambiguity, this patient tending of mystery which lends the poetry its surviving radiance in radically different atmospheres and epochs, such as our own. In this vein, Rilke's extraordinary and sublime proposition, "Is night the sole reality / of a thousand years…" surely deserves no more than our consensual silence.

WILL STONE,
EXMOOR, 2020

POEMS TO NIGHT

The Siblings

O now we have, with what whimpering,
caressed ourselves, shoulders and eyelid.
And night has withdrawn into the rooms
like a wounded beast, in pain through us.

Were you elected from all for me,
was the sister not sufficient?
Lovely as a valley to me was your essence,
and now, too, from the prow of the heavens

it bows down an unfailing apparition
and he takes possession. Where to go?
Alas, with the gesture of mourning
you incline towards me, unconsoled.

(Paris, end of 1913)

When your face consumes me
like tears the one who weeps,
my brow, my mouth propagates
around the features I know for you.

(Paris, turn of the year 1913/14)

Once I took into my hands
your face. The moon fell upon it.
Most unfathomable of things
beneath an overflowing of tears.

Like a willing thing, quietly subsisting,
it was almost like holding something
and yet was no entity in the cold
night that infinitely eludes me.

Oh we stream towards these places,
pressing in on the narrow surface
all the waves of our heart;
yearning and weakness,
and to whom finally do we bear them?

Alas, to the stranger, who misunderstood us,
alas to the other, whom we never found,
to those servants, bound to us,
springtime winds, that with it vanished
and the loser, silence.

(Paris, end of 1913)

From face to face
what rising up.
From the guilty breaks out
sacrifice and forgiveness.

Does the night not blow cool,
splendidly distant,
moving across the centuries.
Raise the area of feeling.
Suddenly the angels
see the harvest.

(Paris, turn of the year 1913/14)

Look, angels sense through space
their infinite feelings.
Our incandescence would be their coolness.
Look, angels glow through space.

Whilst we, who know nothing more,
resist one thing, whilst another occurs in vain,
they stride on, enraptured by their intention,
across their fully formed domain.

(Paris, end of 1913)

Did I not breathe out of midnights,
on such a flood, for the love of you,
that someday you'd come?
For I hoped to appease your countenance
with almost unblemished magnificence,
when in eternal supposition
it rested awhile against mine.
Soundless the space in my outline;
in order to sate your great upward gaze
my blood was mirrored, deepened.

When through the olive trees' pale separation
the night made me stronger with stars,
I rose, stood and turned back,
mastered the realization
I never referred to you later.

Oh what utterance was sown in me
should your smile ever come,
that I survey world space upon you.
But you don't come, or you come too late.
Fall, angels, over this blue
flax field. Angels, angels, reap.

(Paris, end of 1913)

36

So, now it will be the angel
who drinks slowly from my features
the wine-enlightened face.
Thirsting, who signalled you to come?

How thirsty you are. God's cataract
plunges through every vein. How
you can be so thirsty. Abandon
yourself to thirst. (How you have grasped me.)

And I feel, on the current, how your gaze
was parched, and towards your blood
so inclined that I overflow your brows,
those pure ones, completely.

(Paris, end of 1913)

Away, I asked you finally to taste my smile
(if it was not delectable),
in its irresistible approach behind the stars in the East
the angel waits that I make myself limpid.

That no look, no trace of yours limits him,
when he steps into the clearing;
let him be the suffering that afflicted me, wild nature:
and trust in the watering place.

Was I green or sweet to you, let us forget all,
or the shame will overtake us.
Whether I flower or expiate he will calmly appraise,
whom I did not tempt, who came...

(Paris, end of 1913)

Strong, silent, candelabra placed
on the edge: above the night becomes distinct;
we drain ourselves in unlit wavering
before your foundation.

Ours is: not to know the outcome
in the mad inner domain,
you appear out of our impediments
and glow like a high mountain range.

Your desire lies *above* our kingdom,
and we barely grasp what falls upon us;
like the pure night of the spring equinox
you are there, dividing day and day.

Who could ever infuse you
with the mixture that secretly dulls us?
You win glory from all that is monumental,
and we exist in the most trivial.

When we weep, we are nothing but touching,
where we look, we are at the highest awakening;

our smile is far from seducing,
and even when it does seduce, to whom does it attach?

(Anyone.) Angel, is this lament, is this lament?
What is it then, this lament of mine?
Alas, I shriek, with two pieces of wood I strike
without hope anyone will hear.

That I am noisy does not make you louder,
when you don't feel me, because I *am*.
Light, light! Have the stars survey me
more ardently. For I am fading.

(Ronda, beginning of 1913)

Out of this cloud, see: the one that so wildly
    obscures
the star that was a moment past — (and me),
out of those mountainous lands there, which now have
    night,
night winds for a time — (and me),
out of this river on the valley floor, which catches
the gleam of a torn sky-clearing — (and me)
out of me and all of that, to make
a single thing, Lord: out of me and the feeling
with which the flock, returned to the pen,
in acquiescence breathe out the immense black
no-longer-being of the world — me and every light
in the darkness of so many houses, Lord:
to make *one* thing; out of strangers, for
there is not one I know, Lord, and me and me
to make *one* thing; out of the sleepers,
the old men in the hospice, those strangers
who cough gravely in their beds, and out of
sleep-drunk infants at a foreign breast,
out of so much ill-defined and always me,
of nothing but me and all I do not know,

to make the thing, Lord Lord Lord, the thing
which, world-earthly like a meteor,
gathers in its heaviness only the sum
of flight: weighs nothing but arrival.

(Ronda, January 1913)

Why must one go out and take alien things
upon oneself, rather like the porter
who lifts the market basket filled by strangers
from stall to stall, and follows on, loaded down,
and cannot enquire: Lord, why the feast?

Why must one stand there like a shepherd,
so exposed to the excess of influence,
so much part of this space full of happening,
that by leaning against a tree in a landscape
and nothing more, his destiny is fulfilled.

And yet, in his far too widening gaze, he lacks
the calm abatement of the flock. He has
only the world, world in every glance uplifted,
in every inclining world. In him penetrates what
involuntarily belongs to others, inhospitable like
    music
and blind in his blood, transforming, passes.
There in the night he rises, and already from
    outside
has the bird call inside his being

and feels inspirited, because he gathers all the stars
into his vision, heavy — O not like someone
who makes a gift of this night to a beloved,
and regales her with the deeply felt heavens.

(Ronda, January 1913)

But for myself, when I find myself back in the cities'
tangled barbs of turmoil and the flurry
of vehicles around me, solitary,
but for myself, through this impenetrable
    commotion
I recall the sky and the earthy feet of the
    mountains,
the homebound herd entered.
Let me feel of stone,
and let the shepherd's day labour seem possible,
how he roams there, ever browner, and with well-
    judged stone
gathers his flock where it has frayed.
With slow step, not light, his body ruminative,
but when stood, his wonderful bearing. Even now a
    God
could furtively enter that figure and be no less.
Now he lingers, now moves on, as the day
and shadows of clouds
pass through him, as though the space were slowly
thinking thoughts for him.

Let him be what you will, like the quivering night light
in the mantle of the lamp I place myself inside him.
A glow becomes steady. More pure
might Death find its passage.

(Ronda, January 1913)

Straining so hard against the powerful night
they cast their voices into laughter,
that badly burns. O world in revolt ,
so replete with refusal. And yet breathe space,
where the stars drift. Look, all of this has no need
and could surrender to the distance,
move away into the beyond, far from us.
Now, it returns and touches our faces with a look
like the glance of the beloved; it unfurls
before us and perhaps scatters in us
its existence. And we are not worthy.
Perhaps the angels lose some strength,
when after us the starry firmament yields
and hangs here within our mournful fate.
Futility. For who can know? And where
one might become aware: who yet wills
to rest his brow against the nocturnal space
as upon his own window? Who has not renounced this?
Who has not dragged into his primordial element
fakery, falsified, counterfeit nights?
We have abandoned our gods for mouldering waste,
for gods do not beguile. They have being

and nothing but being, abundance of being,
but not a scent, not a sign. Nothing is so mute
as a god's mouth. Sublime as a swan
on its eternity of fathomless surface:
so goes the god, and dives, safeguards his whiteness.

Everything seduces. Even the little bird
coerces us from within his pure foliage,
the flower lacks space and forces a way to us;
what does the wind not crave? Only the god,
like a column, permits passage, distributing
on high where he bears on each side
the light arch of his equanimity.

(Paris, February 1914)

Overflowing skies of squandered stars
splendour over grievance. Rather than into pillows,
weep upwards. Here, at the weeping,
at the ending face,
proliferating, begins
the enraptured world space. Who will interrupt,
if you thrust that way,
the flow? No one. Unless
you suddenly wrestle with the epic course
of those stars approaching you. Breathe.
Breathe the darkness of the earth, and again
look up! Again. Light and faceless,
the depth leans in on you from on high. In contained
    night
the dispersed face grants yours space.

(Paris, April 1913)

Where I once was, or am: there you are treading
over me, you infinite darkness out of light.
And the sublime that you prepare in space,
I draw, unknowable, to my fugitive face.

O Night, take note, the way I regard you,
how my being attempts to go back, give way,
that it dares to launch itself close to you;
can I conceive, that the twice-taken brow
extends over the same streams of upward glance?

Be this nature, be only *one*,
the one bolder nature: this life and
that star I lament unawares:
so will I apply myself, composed like stones
in the purest figure.

(Paris, autumn 1913)

Thoughts of night, raised from intuited experience,
that already passed into the questioning child with
    silence,
slowly I raise you towards my thought — and up, up,
the powerful proof gently receives you.

That you *are* gains affirmation; here, in the crowded
    vessel,
night, added to nights, secretly procreates.
Suddenly: with what feeling stands the infinite, the
    older,
over the sister within me, that, inclined, I shelter.

(Paris, December 1914)

Often I gazed at you in wonder. I stood at the window
    begun yesterday,
stood and marvelled at you. Yet the new city
was denied me and the unpersuaded landscape
darkened, as though I were nothing. Nor did things
    close by
venture to be understood. The street thrust upwards
at the lamp post: I could see it was an alien thing.
Over there a room, sympathetic, clear in the
    lamplight –
I was already a part; this they sensed, closed the
    shutters.
Remained there. Then a child cried. I knew the mothers
in the houses around, of what they are capable – and I
    knew
at once the inconsolable argument behind all weeping.
Or a voice sang out and reached a little beyond
expectation, or down below an old man
who coughed full of reproach, as if his body
were in the right and the gentler world in error. Then
    the hour struck,
but I counted too late, it fell past me.

Like a boy, a stranger, at last deemed worthy to join in
yet drops the ball and knows none of the games
in which the others indulge with such ease,
stands there, looks away – to where?: I stood and
    suddenly
became aware, *you* approached me, played with me, I
    understood,
grown-up night, and I gazed at you enraptured. Where
    the towers
raged and, with fate averted, a city loomed over me
and before me were ranged unknowable mountains
and in the narrowing circle of hungering strangeness
welled the random flickering of my feelings – :
there it was, higher one,
no shame for you, that you know me. Your breath
passed over me, across widening solemn expanses
your smile entered into me.

(Paris, January 1914)

I want to hold out. Act. Go over
as far as you are able. Have you not composed
the faces of shepherds, more greatly even than
in the wombs of princesses, the future's influence and
    boldness
formed the princely expression of countless kings?
When figureheads in the surprised wood of the frozen
    carving
assume their traits in the maritime space where
they forge on in silence:
O, how could a sentient being, who *wills*, who tears
    himself open,
unyielding night, in the end not resemble you.

(Paris, January 1914)

Ah, from an angel's touch falls
into the sea a beam upon a moon,
my heart within, silently striving coral,
dwells there in its youthful branches.

Distress, inflicted on me by an unknown
perpetrator, remains clouded to me,
the current wavers, the current presses on,
depths function and obstructions.

Out of the rigid insentient ancients
the creatures turn, the suddenly elect,
and the eternal silence of all beings
precipitates a tumult of happening.

(Paris, February 1914)

Is pain — as soon as the ploughshare,
labouring, naturally reaches a new layer —
is pain not good? And what can it mean, the last
interrupting us in the depths of such affliction?

How much is still to be borne: when was the time
to achieve that other, lighter feeling?
And yet I know, better than most,
once resurrected, salvation.

(Paris, autumn 1913)

You who super-elevates me with this:
Night, — is it not, that you are granting me
the boundless, more due feeling
than I can sense? Alas, from here

the heavens are powerful, thronged with lions,
who to us remain inscrutable.
No, you cannot know them, for they are timid
and only approach with diffidence.

(Paris, autumn 1913)

Lifting one's eyes from the book, from the close and
   countable lines,
to the consummate night outside:
O how the compressed feelings scatter like stars,
as if a posy of blooms were untied:

Youth of the lighter, inclined swaying of the heavy
and the tenderest of the quieter bow —.
Everywhere craving for connection and nowhere desire,
world too much and earth enough.

(Paris, February 1914)

POEMS TO NIGHT:
DRAFTS

Isn't there a smile? See, what is there
in fields that overflowed from abundance,
is what we bring to a modest blossoming
when we strive in our countenance?

Nocturnal music score never finished:
that reaches your limits, where is the margin?
Where is the voice that has your higher tones?
And in which man is the bass of your abyss?

Is it not granted us, until there
to propagate pure excitation of being,
where grows a superabundance of soul
blissfully happy at disclosed distances?

There it flowed after fall and resistance
of the running, relishing the opened,
in silent arms, the flow diverging
the broad becoming, the worshipper.

(O half of all worlds, unrecognized,
closing over my unrecognized gaze.)

(Paris, November 1913)

Turned upwards to the nourishing one,
I resolved myself to healing night,
my senses have flowed out from me
and the heart propagates namelessly.

(Paris, end of 1913)

Why does the day persuade us,
that here we succumb to privation,
when those powerful nights bow
from creation's worldly harvest?

(Paris, end of 1913)

(To the Angel)

Don't wait for my choice, demand,
you can do it, for you don't require it.
As you throw yourself, soughing,
Impenetrable one, against my gait?
My want was still inclined
to avoid your surge.
But who vouches, in which dykes
when the world sea rises to the sky.

(Paris, turn of the year 1913/14)

How did I hold out this face, that its feeling
rough spaces of strangeness worked through;
there even the poor, delicately peeling birch
might move cities here from the hill.

(Paris, turn of the year 1913/14)

When I feed on your face this way
like the tear on the weeping one,
my brow, my mouth multiply
around the traits, I know of you
(I mean around those similarities
that separate us, because they are double
to broaden out a pure equivalence.)

(Paris, turn of the year 1913/14)

Only now, at the nocturnal hour, am I without fear
and may stand in blossoming gaze,
because you are responsible for your infinite happenings
laying claim to my inadequate face.
Now the resemblance emerges from it

(Paris, turn of the year 1913/14)

FURTHER POEMS
AND SKETCHES
AROUND THE THEME
OF NIGHT

Now the red barberries are already ripening,
ageing asters breathe weakly in the beds.
Who is not rich now that summer is fading
will forever wait and never know self-possession.

Who cannot close his eyes now,
persuaded that an abundance of faces
is only waiting within him till night begins
to rise up in his darkness: —
he has passed away like an old man.

There is nothing left, no day's coming,
and everything that happens lies to him;
you too, my God. And like a stone you are,
daily drawing him down into the deep.

(*From* Das Buch der Pilgerschaft [The Book of Pilgrimage], *1901)*

From a Stormy Night

(Title page)

The night, urged by swelling storms,
how wide it suddenly became –,
there laid out together it remains
in the tiniest creases of time.
Where the stars counter, here it does not end
and does not begin deep in a forest
and not at my countenance
and not with your form.
The lamps falter and do not know:
do we *feign* light?
Is night the sole reality
of a thousand years...

(From The Book of Images, 1906; Berlin-Schmargendorf, January 1901)

Night of the Spring Equinox

A net of swift shadow mesh drags above
garden paths made of moon,
as if something captive were stirring there,
the far distant drew together.

Captive fragrance reluctantly lingers.
Yet all of a sudden it is as if a wave
were tearing the net at a luminescent place,
and all flows there, takes flight, drifts…

Once more breathes the vast night wind
we have long known, in bare trees
standing above, sharp and diamond-like,
in the deep, solemn spaces between
the great stars of a spring night.

(Capri, March 1907)

Stars Behind Olives

Beloved, so much leaves you senseless,
you lean backwards into the pure leafage,
you see the places, are the stars. I believe
the earth is no different to the night.

Behold, as in self-forgetting branches
the next mingles with the nameless;
we are shown this; they do not treat us as guests,
one only takes, amused and refreshed.

However much we have suffered these paths,
we have not worn out the garden,
and hours, greater than we had requested,
feel towards us, lean in on us.

(Capri 1907/Paris 1908)

Nocturnal Walk

Nothing is comparable. For what is not
wholly alone with itself, what can we declare;
we name nothing, we can only endure
and come to understand that here is a gleam,
and there a glance has brushed against us
as if just *that* which dwelled there
were our life. He who opts for resistance
will not receive world. And whoever knows too much
the eternal will slip away from. Sometimes
on such great nights we are as if
out of danger, shared out in equitably lit
parts of the stars. How they cluster.

(Capri, April 1908)

Urban Summer Night

Greyer grows the evening below,
and that is already night,
hung there like warm rags
about the street lamps.
But higher, suddenly imprecise,
has the light bare firewall
of a rear building thrust upwards,
on a night which has full moon
and nothing but moon.

And then a space glides up, spreading
wider, secure and spared,
and the windows on that side
stand white and uninhabited.

(Paris, 1908 or 1909)

Moonlit Night

Path in the garden, deep as a long drink,
quietly in the soft branch an escaping momentum.
Oh and the moon, the moon,
the benches are almost blooming
with her hesitant approach.

Silence, how it presses.
Are you awake now?
Starry and sensing the window facing you.
The wind's hands lay over your nearing face
far-flung night.

(Paris, July 1911)

Like the evening wind
    through shouldered scythes of the reapers
softly goes the angel
    through the guiltless blade of suffering.

Keeps long hours
    at the side of the dark rider,
steers the same course
    as the feelings without name.

Standing as a tower by the sea,
    minded to last forever;
He is what you feel,
    supple at the deepest point of hardness,

that in the rock of woe
    the crowded druse of tears,
for so long water-pure,
    resolved into amethysts.

(Paris, winter 1913/14)

At night I wish to converse with the angel,
ask if he recognizes my eyes.
When he suddenly enquires: Can you see Eden?
Then I must say: Eden is on fire

I will lift my mouth to him,
hard as one who lacks desire.
And if the angel says: Do you know life?
Then I must say: Life devours

If he finds that joy within me
that becomes eternal in his spirit, —
and he takes it, raises it in his hands,
then I must say: joy is madness

(Irschenhausen, September 1914)

Night Sky and Falling Star

The sky, vast, full of joyous retention,
a provisional space, an excess of world.
And we, too far away for the formation,
too near to turn away the future.

There a star falls! And our desire to see it,
with a confused look, ardently conjoined:
What has begun, and what has elapsed?
What is guilty? And what forgiven?

(Muzot, August 1924)

Love the angel is space.
Cosmic space is like granting
loving angel, replete
with the starry gift.

We, in the struggling nights,
we fall from closeness to closeness;
and where the beloved thaws
we are a plunging stone.

But even here where we never
find each other, there are spaces of the angel.
Feel: at a divine double pace
blessedly they transform themselves.

(Muzot, 1922)

From the Periphery: Night

Stars of the night, I have awoken,
do they only overleap today, my face,
or at in the same moment the whole face of my years,
these bridges, resting on columns of light?

Who cares to walk there? For whom am I abyss and
    stream bed,
that he leads me in the widest circle −,
bounds over me and takes me like a bishop on a
    chessboard
and contends his victory?

(Muzot, September 1924)

Strong star, without need of support,
the night might concede to the others
which must first darken so that they brighten.
Star, which, already perfected, submerges,

when stars begin their passage
through the tentatively opening night.
Great star of the priestesses of love,
which, inflamed by a feeling,

transfigured to the last and burning up,
sinks down, where the sun sank:
a thousand times outdistancing
with its pure downfall.

(Muzot, January 1924)

What reaches us with the starlight,
what reaches us,
take the world in your countenance,
but do not take it lightly.

Show the night that you silently received
what she brought.
It is only when you merge into her
that the night knows you.

(Muzot, August 1924)

Earlier, how often, we stayed, star in star
when from the freest constellation
that speech-star detached from the rest and called.
Star in star we marvelled,
He, speaker of the constellation,
I, mouth of my life,
ancillary star to my eye.
And the night, how she granted us
the wakeful rapprochement.

(Val-Mont, February 1926)

BIOGRAPHICAL NOTES

Rainer Maria Rilke

Rainer Maria Rilke (1875–1926) was born in December 1875 in Prague. In 1886 his parents had the child enrolled in the St Pölten military academy, which caused the shy, introspective only child great anxiety. In 1890 he graduated from St Pölten and entered the military secondary school of Mährisch Weisskirchen. In 1894 he published his first collection of poems, *Leben und Lieder* (*Life and Songs*). In the autumn of 1895 Rilke enrolled to study art history, literature and philosophy at the Charles University in Prague. From this point on he was determined to pursue a literary career. At the turn of 1895–96, the twenty-year-old published his second collection, *Larenopfer* (*Offerings to the Lares*), while a third collection, *Traumgekrönt* (*Dream-Crowned*), followed in 1896. Rilke left Prague for the University of Munich, switching his studies to political science, law and Darwinian theory. From 1897 Rilke resided in Berlin

Wilmersdorf, but began to succumb to a lifelong compulsion for travel. In 1898, after a springtime of Italian journeys and the seminal reading of Nietzsche's *The Birth of Tragedy*, Rilke encountered Bremen, Hamburg and, crucially, the artists' colony of Worpswede in northern Germany for the first time. He wrote the *Florenzer Tagebuch* (*Florence Diaries*), *Schmargendorfer Tagebuch* (*Schmargendorf Diaries*) and *Notizen zur Melodie der Dinge* (*Notes on the Melody of Things*). In the spring of 1899, Rilke made an artistically and spiritually groundbreaking journey to Russia with Lou Andreas Salomé, and in 1900 returned for a longer sojourn from May until August. That autumn Rilke revisited Worpswede, where he renewed his friendship with the painter Paula Becker, amongst others, and her friend Clara Westhoff, a former pupil of Rodin, whom he married the following year. In 1902 Rilke set his sights on Paris, with the idea of writing a monograph on Rodin. That same year *The Book of Images* was published. The next twelve years saw Rilke travelling not only widely within Germany and Austria but also making protracted visits to Italy, France, Spain and Egypt. The experiences drawn from these destinations fed into his evolving poetry. In 1905 *The Book of Hours* was published, followed in 1907 by *New Poems*, and finally, after six years of labour, *The Notebooks of Malte Laurids Brigge* in 1910, the great prose work which gave full expression to the poet's spiritual struggle to maintain a solitary existence within

Baudelaire's "fourmillante cité". Rilke would continue to travel throughout his lifetime; most extensively to Italy, Spain and Egypt, but Paris was always the endlessly giving refuge of his life, the engine house and hub from which all else radiated and the required place where the trials enacted with his inner self served to engender a new style of lyrical poetry. But when war broke out in 1914, Rilke was obliged to abandon the French capital for Munich. His possessions were later confiscated from his apartment on the rue Campagne Première by the French authorities; valuable manuscripts and books were never recovered. Moving between Berlin, Vienna and Munich, Rilke suffered the dismal upheaval of war, and the severance of his concentration. But in 1915 he managed to write the fourth Duino elegy and published *Die Fünf Gesänge* (*Five Songs*). In 1916 Rilke worked as a clerk in the war archive and performed military service in Vienna. In this year midway through the war, he presented Rudolf Kassner with the notebook containing the twenty-two poems of the *Poems to Night*. At the midpoint of 1919 Rilke was living in Munich and left the city for a tour of Swiss cities and the alpine region of the Engadine. The next two years saw the poet exploring Bern, Geneva, Locarno, Basel and finally Sion and Sierre. The still-undiscovered canton of Valais captured his heart; it recalled Provence. Seeking a safe harbour, from July 1921 he took up residence in his final refuge, the medieval tower of Château de Muzot above Sierre. 1922 proved an industrious year. Rilke finished the long-running *Duino Elegies* and created in a matter of weeks the *Sonnets to Orpheus*. He completed his translations of Valéry's poems and also wrote *Brief des jungen Arbeiters* (*Letter to a Young Labourer*), whose "Monsieur V" clearly refers to the Belgian poet Émile Verhaeren (1855–1916). At the end of 1923 Rilke, suffering an unnamed malady, visited the sanatorium of Val-Mont sur Territet for the first of several residences. In 1924 he produced a wealth of poems in French, including the sequences *Vergers* (*Orchards*), *Les Quatrains Valaisans* (*The Valais Quatrains*) and *Les Roses* (*The Roses*). In 1925 Rilke was back for a long residence in Paris, but by the end of the year he was ominously reinstalled in Val-Mont. Diagnosed with incurable leukaemia, Rilke, refusing all palliative care, died "his own death" at the sanatorium on 29th December 1926. On 2nd January 1927, Rilke was buried at his own request in the nearby churchyard of Raron. His chosen epitaph reads: "Rose, oh pure contradiction, to be no one's sleep under so many lids."

Will Stone

Will Stone is a writer, poet and literary translator of Franco-Belgian, French and German literature. His first poetry collection, *Glaciation* (Salt, 2007), won the International Glen Dimplex Award for poetry in 2008. Shearsman Books published his most recent collection, *The Sleepwalkers*, in 2016 and will publish his fourth collection in 2020. Will's translations include *Les Chimères* by Gérard de Nerval (Menard, 1999), *To the Silenced: Selected Poems of Georg Trakl* (Arc, 2005), *Emile Verhaeren: Poems* (Arc, 2013), *Georges Rodenbach: Poems* (Arc, 2017) and *Friedrich Hölderlin's Life, Poetry and Madness* by Wilhelm Waiblinger (Hesperus, 2018). His translations of Stefan Zweig with Pushkin Press include *Montaigne* (2015) and *Messages from a Lost World: Europe on the Brink* (2016). Pushkin also published his translation of *The Art of the City: Rome, Florence, Venice* by Georg Simmel (2018) and *Surrender to Night: Collected Poems of Georg Trakl* (2019), as well as producing new editions of *Journeys* by Stefan Zweig (2019), *Rilke in Paris*, including Rilke's "Notes on the Melody of Things", by Maurice Betz/Rainer Maria Rilke (2019) and *On the End of the World* by Joseph Roth (2019). Autumn 2020 saw the publication of *Encounters and Destinies: A Farewell to Europe* by Stefan Zweig and a new edition of Zweig's *Nietzsche*.

Will has contributed poems, translations, essays and reviews to a range of publications including the *London Magazine*, the *TLS*, the *Spectator*, *Apollo* magazine, *RA Magazine*, *The White Review*, *Poetry Review*, *Agenda* and *Modern Poetry in Translation*. His essay on the Belgian painter Léon Spilliaert as illustrator appeared in the catalogue to the exhibition "Léon Spilliaert", at the Royal Academy, London in February 2020. A French translation was included in the catalogue for the same exhibition held at the Musée d'Orsay, Paris from October 2020.

PUSHKIN PRESS

Pushkin Press was founded in 1997, and publishes novels, essays, memoirs, children's books—everything from timeless classics to the urgent and contemporary.

This book is part of the Pushkin Collection of paperbacks, designed to be as satisfying as possible to hold and to enjoy. It is typeset in Monotype Baskerville, based on the transitional English serif typeface designed in the mid-eighteenth century by John Baskerville. It was litho-printed on Munken Premium White Paper and notch-bound by the independently owned printer TJ International in Padstow, Cornwall. The cover, with French flaps, was printed on Rives Linear Bright White paper. The paper and cover board are both acid-free and Forest Stewardship Council (FSC) certified.

Pushkin Press publishes the best writing from around the world—great stories, beautifully produced, to be read and read again.

STEFAN ZWEIG · EDGAR ALLAN POE · ISAAC BABEL
TOMÁS GONZÁLEZ · ULRICH PLENZDORF · JOSEPH KESSEL
VELIBOR ČOLIĆ · LOUISE DE VILMORIN · MARCEL AYMÉ
ALEXANDER PUSHKIN · MAXIM BILLER · JULIEN GRACQ
BROTHERS GRIMM · HUGO VON HOFMANNSTHAL
GEORGE SAND · PHILIPPE BEAUSSANT · IVÁN REPILA
E.T.A. HOFFMANN · ALEXANDER LERNET-HOLENIA
YASUSHI INOUE · HENRY JAMES · FRIEDRICH TORBERG
ARTHUR SCHNITZLER · ANTOINE DE SAINT-EXUPÉRY
MACHI TAWARA · GAITO GAZDANOV · HERMANN HESSE
LOUIS COUPERUS · JAN JACOB SLAUERHOFF
PAUL MORAND · MARK TWAIN · PAUL FOURNEL
ANTAL SZERB · JONA OBERSKI · MEDARDO FRAILE
HÉCTOR ABAD · PETER HANDKE · ERNST WEISS
PENELOPE DELTA · RAYMOND RADIGUET · PETR KRÁL
ITALO SVEVO · RÉGIS DEBRAY · BRUNO SCHULZ · TEFFI
EGON HOSTOVSKÝ · JOHANNES URZIDIL · JÓZEF WITTLIN